When the Music of Sadness Fades

How to Release the Past and Reclaim Your Tomorrow

AF528800

Shyamankar Singhari

When the Music of Sadness Fades

This book is a work of nonfiction, created to provide insight, guidance, and reflection. While every effort has been made to ensure accuracy, the author and publisher make no warranties as to the completeness or applicability of the contents and shall not be held responsible for any damages arising from the use of this material.

Published by WKRISHIND
wkrishind.in

Author: Shyamankar Singhari
Publisher: WKRISHIND

First Edition, 2025

ISBN: 978-81-981954-4-9

Preface

This book was not born from theory, but from lived experience. It grew out of late nights when memories refused to rest, when the echoes of "what could have been" circled endlessly in my mind, and when silence felt louder than words ever could.

When the Music of Sadness Fades is not simply a book about heartbreak; it is about transformation. It is about learning how to sit with pain, to listen to what it teaches, and to slowly rise into a new kind of strength. Each chapter was written with the hope that someone, somewhere—perhaps you—might find comfort in knowing they are not alone in their journey.

The pages ahead weave together moments of reflection, lessons gathered from struggle, and practical steps toward healing. They are not meant to erase your story but to help you rewrite your relationship with it. Sadness may play its song in your life, but like all music, it has an ending. Beyond it lies silence, and beyond that—new melodies waiting to be heard.

If you are holding this book, you may be in the middle of your own song of sadness. My only wish is that as you turn these pages, you begin to sense the gentle fading of that tune and the stirring of something brighter: resilience, renewal, and the quiet strength of a heart learning to love again—without fear.

This book is my offering, my conversation with you. May it be a companion in your hardest hours, and a reminder that even in brokenness, there is beauty.

– Shyamankar Singhari

Dedication

To the quiet souls who carry unspoken stories of love, loss, and healing.
To those who have felt the weight of a name echoing in silence,
and to those who search for light beyond the shadows of memory.

This book is for you—
a reminder that sadness can soften,
that wounds can breathe into wisdom,
and that the heart always knows how to rise again.

— Shyamankar Singhari

Author's Note

This book was not born from imagination, but from life itself.

The story and experiences within these pages were shared with me in trust—whispers of a heart that had walked through love, loss, fear, and the slow, patient return to healing. What I heard was not just pain, but a journey of transformation, of lessons carried in silence, and of resilience hidden beneath broken moments.

I chose to write this book not as a biography, but as a self-help guide inspired by those shared reflections. The "I" and "you" woven throughout are not only the voice of one individual, but the echo of many who have lived through similar emotions. Perhaps you will find pieces of yourself here too.

My role has simply been to listen, to give shape to those fragments, and to turn a deeply personal journey into a path that others may walk with hope and strength.

If you find comfort, clarity, or even a small spark of courage in these pages, then the voice that trusted me will have reached far beyond itself—into you.

Content

Part 1 — The Story

Chapter 1:

The First Sparks of the Heart

A Note to the Reader

What follows is not my own story.
It was entrusted to me—shared in quiet honesty, with the hope that it might one day bring light to others.

These words belong to someone who once carried the weight of unspoken fears and lingering memories. Yet within their story, I found echoes of countless hearts who have felt the same—hesitating to love, fearing loss, and struggling to let go.

I, as the author, have written their experiences not as an isolated tale, but as a mirror for anyone who has ever wrestled with the music of sadness in their own soul. Though the voice is theirs, the journey belongs to all of us.

Note: In the chapters ahead, whenever the word "I" appears, it refers to the person who shared their story with me.

****

I was in 8th grade when I first felt what I thought was love.
She was a relative's daughter — someone I saw

during family gatherings. I didn't know much about relationships, love, or boundaries. I was just a boy, curious and overwhelmed by a feeling I couldn't fully understand.

I tried to get closer to her in ways I now know were wrong – but at that time, I didn't have the maturity to see it. She refused, and I was left confused, frustrated, and quietly hurt.

Years later, when I had grown older, I thanked God for stopping me from crossing a line.
That early rejection became my first teacher: sometimes a "No" is not rejection of *you* – it's protection for *both*.

In 12th grade, it happened again. A new girl, a classmate, caught my attention. I approached her, hoping for something more. She refused. This time, I felt it deeper. My mind wouldn't stop replaying the rejection, and I became mentally unsettled for a while. It wasn't just the refusal – it was the sting of not being chosen.

When I entered college, I met more people. On a trip with friends, I noticed another girl. But this story played out the same way. She didn't choose me either. There was another boy in our group – charming, good-looking, skilled at getting attention. I watched him attract her while I faded into the background. I told myself he was just "lucky," but deep down I felt small.

Looking back, I realize something important:

Rejection is a mirror.
It reflects not just how others see you, but also how you see yourself. Every time I was turned away, my mind whispered the same lie: *You're not enough.*

The truth? I was enough. I just didn't believe it yet.

When we're young, our hearts are fragile. We think love will come quickly, easily, and perfectly — like in the movies. But real love doesn't work like that. It takes maturity, patience, and the courage to be okay when things don't go our way.

If you're reading this and you've faced rejection, I want you to remember:

- A "No" is not the end of your story.
- Sometimes people refuse not because you're unworthy, but because they're walking a different path.
- Your value is not defined by who chooses you, but by how you choose yourself.

💡 Self-Help Exercise:

Take a moment to list 3 times in your life when someone's "No" later turned out to be protection for you. Think about what could have gone wrong if it had been a "Yes."

****

"As the sparks of first feelings flicker, they leave traces that shape our earliest understanding of love, guiding us into the lessons of our first crushes and school days."

Chapter 2:
The Love That Never Fully Began

"The first sparks of affection often lead us into uncharted emotions, teaching lessons we didn't realize we needed."

By the time I reached my graduation years, I thought I understood relationships a little better. I had learned that attraction alone wasn't enough — you needed connection, patience, and mutual interest.

That's when I met her. Not in person, but on Instagram.
At first, she was just someone helping me with information about a college where I wanted to do my post-graduation. She replied to my messages faster than anyone else. I didn't think much of it at first — she was simply being helpful.

But over the months, our conversations grew longer, deeper. We talked about admissions, studies, life, and little everyday things. Somewhere along the way, my heart made a decision my mind wasn't ready for: *I liked her.*

I proposed. She said no.
It wasn't harsh, just firm — she didn't want to be in a relationship.
I accepted it… or at least I thought I did.

As time passed, I found myself circling back. The connection we had, even in words on a screen, kept pulling me. I asked again. And again. And again. Most times, she refused politely. But one day, unexpectedly, she said yes.

For two days, I thought I had finally arrived where I had always wanted to be. But on the third day, she ended it. Her reason? "You're too emotional, and when the time comes, you won't be able to leave me." She also told me to find someone else.

That breakup wasn't long, but it was deep.
It was the first time I realized something about myself — I wasn't just looking for love, I was looking for permanence. And in a world where so much is temporary, that made my heart a fragile place.

After that, I drifted. I chatted with a few other girls online, even met one in person who once spent the night beside me — though nothing physical happened. Still, the thought of moving on felt impossible. My mind kept going back to *her*.

Long-distance relationships are strange things. You don't share daily routines, you don't pass each other in hallways, but you can still feel someone's presence everywhere. And when it ends, it's like losing something invisible but heavy.

💡 Self-Help Insight:

Long-distance love can often feel more intense because it exists in imagination as much as in reality. We fill in the gaps with our hopes and idealized images of the other person. This can make letting go harder — not because of who they are, but because of the *version* of them we've built in our minds.

Reflective Prompt:

Write down what you miss most about someone from your past. Then ask yourself: *Is this about who they really were, or who I wanted them to be?*

****

"Even as we learn and grow, fear quietly settles in, coloring how we see ourselves and others in relationships yet to come."

Chapter 3:

The Fear That Stays

"Fear, though invisible, shapes the choices we make and the paths we take in love and life."

My parents talk about marriage often now.
They see it as the next step in my life — a natural, expected part of adulthood.
But when the topic comes up, my mind doesn't picture a future with someone new.
It drifts back to *her*.

I imagine a married life with the girl who broke up with me after just two days.
I know there's no real chance of it happening, but hope is a stubborn thing.
It lives in the corners of your mind even when reason tries to chase it away.

There's another thought that haunts me:
What if the woman I marry has already been physically intimate with someone else?

I know — everyone has a past. I understand this logically.
But emotions don't always follow logic.

Somewhere deep inside, there's a fear that this would make me less special in her life. That maybe I'd always be compared to someone before me.

This fear isn't just about the future — it's rooted in the past.
It comes from a pattern of not being chosen, of being replaced or overlooked.
It's about trust, yes, but also about my own sense of worth.

One day, while still connected with *her*, she said something strange in Hindi:
"*Kisi na kisi ke saath to hoga*" — implying that she would eventually be with someone.
I laughed it off at the time, but the sentence stuck with me like a thorn.
It made me imagine things I didn't want to imagine.

Later, a misunderstanding with her brother over Instagram only made things worse.
I followed him, thinking he knew about me and would be open. We even chatted briefly, but his last message — "*Bhai tu hai kaun, aur mujhe kaise jaanta hai?*" — hit me hard.
When I tried to clarify, I found I had been blocked by both of them.

Self-Help Insight:

Fear often grows in silence. The less we know, the more our mind fills in the blanks – and rarely in a positive way. That's why clear communication and self-trust are essential in relationships. Without them, imagination becomes your worst enemy.

Practical Exercise – Rewriting the Story in Your Head:

1. Write down the fearful thought (e.g., What if my partner has been with someone before me?).

2. Underneath, write a neutral fact (e.g., Everyone has a past; it doesn't define my present with them.).

3. Then, write an empowering version (e.g., I am worthy of love and trust regardless of someone's past.).
   Repeat this whenever fear resurfaces.

****

"Recognizing fear is the first step, but taking small steps toward change brings the real shift in our hearts and actions."

Chapter 4:

Small Steps, Big Shifts

"Every conscious step we take toward understanding ourselves creates ripples that influence our relationships."

Healing doesn't always begin with grand, cinematic moments.
Sometimes, it starts with small, quiet decisions – like deleting an app.

I didn't just uninstall Instagram from my phone.
I deleted my account completely.
It wasn't about running away from the world – it was about reclaiming my own mental space.
No more late-night scrolling through her profile.
No more checking who she followed, who liked her posts, or who commented.

Truecaller history? Deleted.
Anything that could pull me back into an emotional spiral – gone.

These steps didn't erase my feelings instantly.
But they made one important change: I stopped adding fuel to the fire in my head.
I learned that sometimes, healing isn't about

"moving on" immediately – it's about removing the things that keep pulling you back.

There was also something else I realized – I didn't want to connect with someone new right away.
Not because I had lost faith in love entirely, but because I was still carrying fear.
Fear of being hurt again.
Fear of opening up only to be compared, rejected, or replaced.

This fear wasn't a weakness; it was a sign that I needed to heal *before* I tried again.
Jumping into a new relationship without addressing old wounds would only repeat the same cycle.

💡 Self-Help Insight:

Cutting off emotional triggers is a form of self-respect.
It tells your mind, "*I care enough about myself to protect my peace.*"
But remember – removing triggers is step one.
Step two is filling that empty space with healthier habits, creative projects, and supportive people.

For me, that "filling the space" came through writing.
I've been an author for a while, but for some reason, I couldn't solve my own emotional puzzle with words – until now.
After talking through everything and seeing patterns in my own story, I decided:
I would write a book.
Not just for others, but for myself.
A self-help journey, built from my own scars, lessons, and hopes.

Practical Exercise – Your Trigger-Free Zone:

1. Make a list of all people, apps, and habits that pull you back into sadness or anxiety.

2. Decide which to remove completely and which to limit.

3. Fill that time and space with one creative or growth-based activity each week.

****

"Each step forward is accompanied by waves of emotion–letting them flow freely allows us to rise stronger after the tears."

Chapter 5:
Cry, Then Rise

"Allowing yourself to feel deeply is the first act of true healing."

There's a strange truth about emotions – sometimes you can't move forward until you let them out.
Not with forced positivity. Not with distractions.
But with an honest, unapologetic release.

For me, that meant tears.
The kind that come when a song hits just the right note and unlocks the dam you've been holding shut.

When I told myself, "*It's okay to cry*," I stopped feeling weak for doing it.
I understood that crying wasn't the end of strength – it was the beginning of it.
After the tears, my chest felt lighter, my breathing easier.

That's why I created my own Hindi **"Cry-and-Heal" playlist** for the days when emotions felt too heavy to hold inside.

Playlist:

1. *Channa Mereya* - for the pain of letting go.

2. *Agar Tum Saath Ho* - for the longing that never fully fades.

3. *Kabira (Encore)* - for bittersweet acceptance.

4. *Phir Le Aaya Dil (Reprise)* - for the quiet ache of remembering.

5. *Tadap Tadap* - for when the hurt needs to be felt in full before it can leave.

These songs didn't "fix" me, but they helped me stop resisting my emotions.
I learned that healing isn't about silencing sadness — it's about allowing it to pass through without getting stuck.

💡 Self-Help Insight:

Emotional release is a cleansing process.
Whether it's tears, writing, music, or even silent

reflection, it's better to let feelings out than to bury them alive inside you.

Practical Exercise — Build Your Cry-and-Heal Routine:

1. Choose 3–5 songs that resonate deeply with your current emotions.

2. Set aside a quiet 20–30 minutes where you can be alone and undisturbed.

3. Listen intentionally, allowing tears or memories to surface without judgment.

4. After the session, write one paragraph about what you felt — not to analyze, but to acknowledge.

****

"After the storm of crying, we discover that love without fear is possible when we trust ourselves and embrace vulnerability."

Chapter 6:

Love Without Fear

"Courage grows from understanding, and vulnerability becomes strength."

When you've been hurt before, it's tempting to build walls so high no one can reach you.
It feels safe at first.
But after a while, you realize you're not just keeping others out – you're locking yourself in.

I learned that fear of love is not really fear of love itself – it's fear of the pain we think might follow.
It's fear of betrayal, rejection, and disappointment.
And while those risks are real, they are not guarantees.

I promised myself:
When I decide to open my heart again, I will do it *with awareness*, not with blind hope.
That means:

- I will know my own worth before seeking validation from someone else.

- I will set boundaries early, not as walls, but as doors that open and close with respect.
- I will allow trust to grow naturally, not force it to appear in a day.

💡 Self-Help Insight:

You can't erase the possibility of being hurt, but you can prepare yourself to handle it in a healthy way.
Resilience in love comes from knowing that your self-worth doesn't depend on someone else's choice to stay or leave.

Practical Exercise — Your Love Readiness Checklist:

Before entering a new relationship, ask yourself:

1. Have I healed enough from past wounds to give without fear?
2. Do I trust myself to walk away if I'm disrespected?
3. Can I be happy in my own company before adding someone else's?

4. Do I know my non-negotiables – the values and behaviors I won't compromise on?

If you can answer "yes" to most of these, you're closer than you think to loving without fear.

A Note on Marriage Pressure:

Family expectations can be strong, but marriage isn't a race.
It's not about finding someone quickly – it's about finding someone right for you.
Choosing under pressure can lead to regret, while waiting for alignment can lead to lasting peace.

****

From resilience to her reaching out again

Resilience gives us strength, but strength does not erase our longing. Sometimes, just when we begin to heal, life sends a test in the form of an unexpected message or a familiar name on our screen. These moments remind us that moving on is not a straight line–it is a journey full of pauses, returns, and unexpected turns.

Chapter 7:
From Story to Strength

"Every narrative, every experience carries lessons that can empower us if we choose to learn from them."

When I first began telling my story, I thought it was a record of failed connections and heartbreaks.
But looking back, I see something different – I see growth.

Every "no" I received taught me about boundaries.
Every rejection taught me about self-worth.
Every period of loneliness taught me about the strength in standing alone.

This book is not just about relationships.
It's about the deeper truth that **our value is not determined by who chooses us, but by how we choose ourselves**.
And when we finally choose ourselves – with all our scars, lessons, and still-unfolding dreams – we step into a kind of freedom that no one can take away.

💡 Final Self-Help Insight:

Healing is not about forgetting the past — it's about building a future that isn't controlled by it.
Your past experiences can remain part of your story without being the driver of your decisions.

Practical Closing Exercise — Your Personal Declaration:

Write down (and repeat daily) a statement that affirms your worth and vision.
Here's an example:

"I am worthy of love, respect, and joy.
My past does not define me.
I will walk into my future with courage, trust, and self-respect."

A Message to the Reader:

If you've read this far, you might be someone who has been through your own storms.
Maybe you've been told "no" too many times.
Maybe you've feared opening your heart again.
This book is proof that even when fear feels permanent, hope is always waiting.

And remember — the strength you're looking for is already within you.
Sometimes, all you need is the courage to use it.

****

From her contact to imagined stories replaying in the mind

Even after conversations end, the mind continues to write its own chapters. It plays old words on repeat, invents new endings, and paints pictures of what could have been. These inner stories can be comforting or painful, but either way, they become part of our healing.

"Now that we've shared the story of love, longing, and lessons learned, it's time to turn inward. Understanding how the mind and heart process attachment, fear, and loss will give us the tools to navigate emotions with clarity and strength."

Part 2 — Understanding the Mind and Heart

Chapter 8:
The Stories We Replay

"Replayed stories are not weakness; they are the mind's attempt to process unresolved emotions."

When the mind holds on to someone, it does not let go easily.
Even when reality is clear, the heart still weaves imagined moments.
We picture bumping into them again.
We rehearse conversations that never happened.
We feel the tears in daydreams that only exist inside us.

This is not weakness.
It is the heart's way of seeking closure.

Why We Replay Scenarios

Our mind wants to "*finish the story*" that ended without answers.

These imagined scenes allow us to express the words or emotions we never had the chance to share.

But replaying too much can trap us in pain instead of releasing it.

Turning Imagination Into Healing

Instead of resisting these scenes, we can use them as a healing tool.

Notice the Scene

When your mind drifts into "*what if*" moments, pause and acknowledge it.
Say to yourself: "*This is my heart looking for closure.*"

Write It Out

Describe the scene fully – the setting, the words, the emotions.
Let your tears fall onto the page if they must.

Shift the Ending

Instead of leaving the story open-ended, give it a gentle close.
Walk away in your imagination not with bitterness, but with peace.
Let your version of the story end in strength, not longing.

The Power of Rewriting

When we take control of these inner stories, we take control of our healing.
We stop being victims of memories and become authors of our closure.

Because the truth is this:
We cannot always change what happened in reality.
But we can always decide how the story ends in our heart.

💡 Practical Exercise:

Choose one recurring "*imagined moment*" with someone from your past.
Write it out in detail. Then rewrite the ending so that you leave with peace, dignity, and self-respect.

Repeat this whenever a new scene comes up. Over time, your heart will stop clinging to old stories, because it will finally feel them complete.

****

"By noticing these inner narratives, we reclaim control over our emotional world and begin to write our own endings."

Chapter 9:

Reclaiming Your Story

"Awareness of the stories we replay is the first step toward reclaiming power over our emotions."

Every heartbreak leaves behind more than silence.
It leaves a story.
A story we tell ourselves about why it happened,
about who we are,
about whether we are worthy of love.

Too often, that story becomes one of rejection.
We say: "*I wasn't good enough.*"
We believe: "*Others are chosen, not me.*"
We carry: "*Maybe I am destined to be left behind.*"

But what if that is not the truth?
What if rejection is not the final chapter, but the beginning of a new one?

The Trap of Rejection

Rejection feels personal.
It stings not only because someone walked away,

but because it echoes our deepest fear –
that maybe we are unlovable.

But here is the truth:
Rejection often says more about the other person's readiness,
their desires, their path,
than it does about your worth.

It is not a verdict on your value.
It is a redirection toward something better aligned with your life.

Choosing Yourself

When someone else says "*no*",
you still have the power to say "*yes*" to yourself.

Yes to healing.
Yes to growth.
Yes to becoming the kind of person who no longer needs someone else's approval to feel complete.

You are not defined by who accepts or rejects you.
You are defined by how you rise after the fall.

Shifting the Story

Instead of telling yourself: "I *was not chosen.*"
Begin telling yourself: "I *am choosing myself.*"

Instead of saying: "I was abandoned."
Say: "I am being guided to a better path."

Your story is not about loss,
but about strength.
Not about what ended,
but about what is beginning within you.

The Author of Your Life

Every time you change the story you tell yourself,
you reclaim your power.

No one else gets to be the sole narrator of your life.
Not the one who rejected you.
Not the one who left.
Not even the one who forgot you.

The pen is in your hand.
You are the author.
You decide how the next chapter unfolds.

💡 **Practical Exercise:**

Take a painful memory of rejection.
Write down the story you've been telling yourself about it.
Then rewrite the story in a way that empowers you.
Read it every day until it feels like truth.

✨ Because here's the secret:
Healing is not about erasing the past.
It's about reclaiming the story of who you are becoming.

****

Reclaiming your story is not only about rewriting the inner narratives of rejection and self-doubt.
It also means reclaiming the moments in life that once belonged to pain.

Because memories don't only live in our minds – they live in dates, in anniversaries, in places, in rituals.
A birthday, an old message notification, or even a yearly festival can feel like a door opening to the past.

And while we cannot erase the calendar, we can choose how we honor it.
The same day that once pulled us back into sorrow can, with intention, become a day of renewal.

This is where the journey continues – from rewriting the inner story, to transforming the outer rituals that shape our emotional world.

"Once we take charge of our story, even painful dates and memories can be transformed into moments of renewal and growth."

Chapter 10:

Transforming Dates of Pain into Days of Renewal

"Painful memories, when approached with intention, can be turned into lessons of resilience and hope."

There are certain dates that never leave us.
A birthday. An anniversary. A day when someone walked away.

For me, **19th September** became one such date. It was her birthday – the person I once loved deeply, the person I hoped would stay, but didn't. Even after she left my life, my heart wanted to mark the day every year. It whispered to me: "*Go to the temple, remember her, keep the connection alive.*"

At first, this felt like devotion. But I realized it was also a trap. By visiting the temple only for her, I was keeping myself tied to a memory, not allowing my heart to heal.

That's when a thought came to me: What if I change the meaning of the ritual?

Instead of going to the temple for **her**, I could go for **me**.

A New Ritual

On that day, I carry a small flower or diya to the temple.
At the gate, I pause and whisper:
"I step inside with love. I leave behind my pain."

I make my offering, but not in her name. Instead, I pray for three blessings:

1. **Peace of mind** - freedom from the constant replay of memories.

2. **Emotional strength** - to face rejection and loss without breaking.

3. **Openness** - to welcome new joys, people, and experiences into my life.

When I leave the temple, I drop a leaf or flower behind me, silently saying:
"With this, I release my attachment. I carry only love and peace within me."

And at night, I light a small diya at home, telling myself:
"This day is not for sorrow. This day is for healing."

The Lesson

Painful dates do not have to control us. We can transform them.
Instead of anniversaries of loss, they can become **milestones of renewal**.

Every time my heart wants to make 19th September about her, I gently remind it:
"*This day belongs to me now. This is my day of healing.*"

Affirmation for Renewal

"I release the past with love,
I free my heart from pain.
May peace and strength guide me,
Like sunlight after rain.
This day is not for sorrow,
But for healing to begin.
I choose to grow, I choose to shine,
With calmness deep within."

Reflection Exercise: Reclaiming Your Dates

Take a quiet moment with a notebook and pen.

1. **Identify Your Date of Pain**
    - Write down one date that still brings up heavy emotions for you (a breakup, a loss, or a memory of rejection).

2. **Acknowledge the Memory**
    - In a few sentences, describe what happened and why this date feels heavy. Don't censor yourself – let the emotions come out.

3. **Choose a New Meaning**
    - Now, write how you want to **redefine this date.**
      For example:
        - "This will be my day of self-care."
        - "This will be the day I visit a temple for inner peace."
        - "This will be the day I light a candle for healing."

4. **Create a Ritual**
    - Decide on one small action you will do every year on this date.
      (It could be visiting a temple, writing in your journal, helping

someone in need, or simply spending time in nature.)

5. **Seal It with an Affirmation**
   - End by writing and repeating: "This day no longer controls me. I transform it into light and strength."

🌸 Remember: the goal isn't to erase the memory, but to **change its power over you.**

****

From rituals of letting go to forgiveness

Rituals help us release the weight of the past, but true peace requires something deeper. Beyond ceremonies and symbolic acts lies forgiveness—the quiet courage to set ourselves free from resentment.

"With clarity about the past, we confront the fear of love while still holding hope for authentic connection."

Chapter 11:

The Fear of Love, the Hope of Connection

"Love often appears with fear, but hope remains our guiding light."

Even as we heal, a quiet fear often remains: "What if I open my heart again, and it breaks the same way?"

This fear is natural.
When love has once been tied to rejection or uncertainty, the heart becomes cautious, even suspicious.

The Fear of Intimacy

For many, the thought of entering a new relationship is shadowed by questions:

- What if I'm not enough?
- What if they leave me?
- What if their past makes me feel insecure?

This fear doesn't mean you are weak.
It means you value connection so deeply that you want to protect it from pain.

Holding Both Fear and Hope

Healing does not mean erasing fear – it means learning to carry it alongside hope.
The truth is, every bond involves risk.
No love story comes with guarantees.

But the very act of choosing to love again, even with fear, is an act of courage.

Building Trust with Yourself

Before you can fully trust another, you must learn to trust yourself.
To know that even if love ends, you will not end.
To believe that your worth is not defined by someone's acceptance or rejection.

Practical Step: Small Acts of Openness

You don't have to rush into deep relationships to practice trust.
Start small:

- Share your thoughts with a friend.
- Allow someone to support you when you're struggling.
- Accept kindness without doubting it.

Each small act rebuilds your faith in connection.

From Fear to Freedom

The opposite of fear is not fearlessness.
It is freedom – the freedom to risk love, knowing you will be okay no matter what.

And with that freedom, relationships stop being cages of expectation.
They become gardens where both people can grow – without fear, but with courage.

💡 Exercise:

Write down your top three fears about future relationships.
Next to each, write a truth that balances it. Example:

- Fear: "What if they leave me?"
- Truth: "If they do, I will still be whole, and I will rise again."

****

"Knowing the delicate balance between attachment and self-preservation allows us to love without losing ourselves."

The next challenge is even deeper:
When love does arrive, how do we make sure we don't lose ourselves in it?
This is where the journey continues – from simply daring to love again, to learning how to love in a way that protects your identity, your dignity, and your inner peace.

From forgiveness to fear of trusting again

Forgiveness opens the door to healing, but stepping through that door often stirs new fears. If we could be hurt once, what stops it from happening again? This fear of trust becomes the next mountain to climb.

Chapter 12:

Love Without Losing Yourself

"Preserving our identity while loving others is the foundation of healthy relationships."

One of the biggest lessons after heartbreak is this:
You cannot heal by making another person your entire world.

Love is beautiful, but it should not come at the cost of your identity.

Why We Lose Ourselves in Love

When we finally find someone who accepts us, we sometimes cling too tightly.
We start shaping our choices, our time, even our dreams around them.
Not because we are weak, but because we fear losing them.

But love born from fear turns into dependency – and dependency always breeds pain.

The Balance of Togetherness and Independence

Healthy love is not two halves becoming one.
It is two wholes walking side by side.

Each person keeps their individuality, yet chooses to share their life.

When you keep your passions, your friendships, your self-respect alive, your love grows richer. Because then, you are not loving out of need – you are loving out of abundance.

Protecting Your Inner Ground

Think of your heart as a garden.
If you let someone else decide all the seeds to plant, you'll end up with a garden that doesn't feel like yours.
But if you keep tending your own flowers – your values, your creativity, your inner peace – then anyone who enters will see the beauty you've already cultivated.

Practical Step: The "Self-Check" in Relationships

Whenever you feel too absorbed in someone else, pause and ask:

- What did I enjoy today that was *just mine*?
- Did I silence my voice to please them?
- Am I still following my own dreams, or only theirs?

Answer honestly. If you notice imbalance, gently bring yourself back.

Love That Frees, Not Binds

The greatest love does not consume.
It gives space to breathe, space to grow, and space to be.

When you learn to hold on lightly — not with fear, but with trust — love stops being a prison and becomes a blessing.

💡 Exercise:

List three activities, passions, or dreams that are *only yours.*
Commit to nurturing them, even if you enter a relationship.
Remind yourself: "I am whole on my own. Love adds to my life, but it does not define my life."

****

In the last chapter, we learned how to let go of the heavy stories we keep replaying — the old memories that trap us in the past.
But even when we release those stories, the journey is not over.

Because sometimes, without warning, their name itself returns to us.

It appears in our thoughts while we are working, eating, or even praying.
Along with it come fears and imaginations – some painful, some hopeful.

This is the next stage of healing:
learning how to respond when their name appears in the mind, and how to transform those sudden storms into moments of strength.

"Even when we move forward, their presence may suddenly appear in our minds, testing our trust and self-control."

Chapter 13:

When Their Name Appears

"Thoughts of someone special can surface uninvited, stirring emotions and fears we thought were behind us."

Sometimes, no matter how hard we try, their name suddenly appears in our mind.
Not because we want it, but because the heart is still holding on.

Along with the name come storms of imagination:

- What if she is with someone else?
- What if she chooses a person like the ones I dislike?
- What if I was never enough?

And yet, another voice speaks too:

- No, I believe in her.
- I believe in God.
- This will not happen.

The Clash of Fear and Faith

This is the heart's battlefield.
Fear paints images of betrayal.
Faith whispers trust and dignity.

Neither is fully true. They are only voices of the mind.
Reality exists outside these battles, in the present moment — where we are safe, alive, and still growing.

How to Respond When Their Name Appears

1. **Pause and Recognize**
   When the thought comes, don't fight it.
   Say softly: "*This is fear, not fact.*"

2. **Anchor Yourself**
   Replace the fear with something grounding:

   - A prayer.

   - A memory of peace, like the quiet of a temple.

   - Or a mantra: "I release what weighs me down, and I carry only what helps me grow."

3. **Release the Name**
   Write their name on a piece of paper.

Look at it. Feel the weight.
Then draw a single line through it, not in anger, but in peace.
This act tells the heart: "I *acknowledge, and I release.*"

Why This Matters

Our pain is not really about what they are doing now.
It is about what we fear, and what we imagine.

The truth is: we do not control their choices.
But we can always control what we hold in our heart.

And every time we release a painful image, we clear space for healing.

💡 Practical Exercise

Next time her name appears suddenly:

1. Say to yourself: "This is only a thought, not truth."
2. Write her name once.
3. Draw a line through it with peace.
4. Whisper: "I release her to God's path, and I walk my own."

“A thought is only a cloud – I am the sky that remains.”

****

In the last chapter, we explored how the mind swings between fear and faith – one moment imagining betrayal, the next moment holding on to trust. That inner conflict shows how powerful our thoughts can be.

But the mind rarely stops there. Even when trust begins to settle in, new doubts arrive in disguise: *What if she meets someone else? What if I lose her again? What if the future hurts me more than the past?*

These *“what if” thoughts become another prison, one built not from reality, but from imagination.*

And so, *in the next chapter, we turn toward these fears. We will see them for what they truly are – stories of the mind, not facts of life – and learn how to step out of their grip.*

From doubt and faith into fears about her future in the city

Trust *and doubt are never silent—they* echo *inside us even when we try to quiet them.* And *sometimes, that echo takes shape in new worries:*

not just about what happened, but about what might happen as life moves forward.

“These intrusive thoughts often trap us in a ‘what if’ scenario, a mental prison that keeps us tethered to fear.”

Chapter 14:
The Prison of "What If"

"What-if scenarios are mental loops that exaggerate fear and uncertainty."

The mind is restless.
It does not like uncertainty.
When answers are missing, it invents them.

That is why "what if" thoughts appear so often.
What if she is with someone else?
What if someone proposes to her?
What if I lose her completely?

These are not truths.
They are fears dressed as possibilities.
They arrive not because of reality,
but because the heart is still trying to control what it cannot.

Why "What If" Thoughts Hurt

Every time we enter this cycle, we hand our peace to the unknown.
We let imagination decide our emotions.
And in doing so, we suffer twice –
once from the loss that already happened,
and again from the stories our mind invents.

But sometimes, a memory interrupts the fear.
Her words echo:
"So *you don't have trust...?*"

And in that moment, we realize the truth.
The problem is not her life.
The problem is our mind's attempt to predict it.

Choosing Trust Over Fear

Trust is not about her.
It is about us.
It is about trusting that life unfolds as it should, and that we will be okay – regardless of what she does or does not do.

When we replace fear with trust, the imagined storms quiet down.
Instead of picturing betrayals that never happened,
we can picture her simply living her life,
while we continue building ours.

A Practice for Releasing "What Ifs"

1. **Catch the thought.** Notice the "what if" as soon as it enters.

2. **Name it.** Whisper: "This is fear, not fact."

3. **Replace it.** Imagine her peacefully working, just as you once did – not as your possession, but as a person with her own path.

4. **Return home.** Bring your focus back to your own life, your own healing, your own growth.

The Lesson

We do not need to fight the "what ifs."
We only need to see them for what they are – attempts of the mind to control the uncontrollable.

And once we see clearly,
we can step out of the prison of imagined pain
and into the freedom of real peace.

💡 Practical Exercise:

Each time a "what if" thought appears, write it down in one column.
Next to it, in another column, write the words:
"*This is fear, not fact.*"
Then replace it with a grounding truth, such as:
"*Her choices are hers. My peace is mine.*"

Over time, you will train your mind to stop fueling fear and to return to calm.

****

"When memories return in loops, it is a natural process of the mind trying to process, yet there are ways to break free."

Chapter 15:
When Memories Return in Loops

"Recurring memories remind us of unresolved emotions and the need for conscious reflection."

The mind does not heal in a straight line.
It circles.
It revisits.
It returns to the same memories again and again, like a bird flying back to a broken nest.

You may find yourself replaying conversations you had months ago.
You may imagine different outcomes — "If only I had said this," or "If only I had done that."
And sometimes, the same painful thoughts appear in new disguises.

This does not mean you are weak.
It does not mean you are failing to heal.
It simply means your heart is still trying to process what happened.

Why the Loops Happen

- **Unfinished business**: The relationship ended without the closure your heart wanted. So the mind creates its own versions.

- **Emotional residue**: Love leaves imprints. The brain, wired for attachment, takes time to let go of old patterns.
- **The search for meaning**: When pain feels unfair, the mind looks for explanations – even if they hurt more.

The Risk of Endless Loops

When memories replay too often, they stop helping and start hurting.
Instead of bringing closure, they dig the wound deeper.
Instead of teaching, they trap you in the same emotional cage.

Breaking the Loop

You cannot stop a thought from coming. But you can stop it from staying.

Here are three gentle practices:

1. **Name the Loop**
   When the same thought comes back, whisper to yourself:
   "This is just a loop. I have been here before."
   Naming it weakens its power.

2. **Ground in the Present**
   Touch something around you – your desk, your cup, the earth beneath your

feet.
Breathe deeply and remind yourself:
"That memory is not happening now. This moment is safe."

3. **Reframe the Story**
   Instead of letting the loop play the same painful ending, give it a new one.
   Imagine yourself walking away peacefully.
   Imagine yourself smiling, stronger, free.

Healing is Spiral, Not Straight

Think of healing not as a line but as a spiral.
You may pass by the same memories again, but each time you are a little stronger, a little wiser.
The loop does not mean you are stuck. It means you are still moving – slowly, quietly – toward freedom.

Practical Exercise:

Next time a looping thought comes, write it down in one sentence.
Then underneath, write: "I *release this thought. I choose peace.*"
Repeat daily. Over time, the loop will lose its grip.

****

"In learning to interrupt these loops, we notice the constant battle between heart and logic, between desire and reason."

Chapter 16:

The Battle Between Heart and Logic

"Our hearts long for connection, but our minds remind us of reality's boundaries."

Even after understanding your feelings and practicing healing exercises, the mind and heart often remain at odds. Logic tells you one thing: "*She is in the past. Focus on your life. Move forward.*" But the heart insists: "*I miss her. What if things were different?*"

Understanding the Battle

This tension is natural. The heart remembers emotions vividly, while the mind tries to analyze and control them. Trying to force the heart to "follow logic" often results in frustration, guilt, or overthinking.

Listening Without Judging

The key is not to fight your heart or suppress your thoughts. Acknowledge them:

- Recognize the emotional surge without labeling it as "wrong."

- Pause and breathe before reacting or letting the mind spiral.

Aligning Heart and Logic

1. **Identify the Truth** – Ask yourself gently: "*What is real in this moment?*" Facts, not fears, guide logic.

2. **Validate Emotions** – Allow the heart its feelings. Write them down or speak them aloud. Emotional validation strengthens resilience.

3. **Choose Your Action** – Once the heart is heard, let logic guide what to do next. For instance, redirecting focus to personal growth, friendships, or goals.

Practical Exercise

Next time you notice a memory or fear surfacing, pause. Name the thought. Ask: "Is *this heart or logic speaking?*" Then decide: "*What choice serves me best right now?*"

The Path Forward

The battle between heart and logic will not vanish overnight. But with practice, it becomes less of a conflict and more of a dialogue. Your heart learns to trust that the mind's guidance is not about ignoring feelings but about channeling them into strength.

💡 **Reflection Prompt:**

Think of one recent moment when your heart and logic clashed. How could you acknowledge both sides without guilt or frustration? Write down your approach. Over time, these moments become stepping stones toward inner harmony.

****

"When logic feels harsh, faith and spiritual anchors can provide calm, stability, and guidance toward healing."

"Having explored the patterns of thought, emotional loops, and the delicate balance between heart and logic, the next step is to cultivate healing. By leaning on faith, solitude, and self-awareness, we can transform pain into growth and redefine what love truly means."

Part 3 — The Path to Healing

Chapter 17:

The Role of Faith and Spiritual Anchors

"Faith, prayer, and spiritual practices can act as stabilizing forces when uncertainty threatens our peace."

When the heart feels heavy and the mind is restless, turning to faith can provide stability. Faith is not about denying emotions; it is about finding a guiding light when life feels uncertain.

Why Faith Matters

Faith, whether in God, the universe, or a higher principle, helps anchor us during emotional storms. When trust in people wavers, faith reminds us that there is a larger plan beyond our immediate understanding. It does not erase pain, but it gives perspective and hope.

Practical Ways to Strengthen Spiritual Anchors

1. **Prayer and Meditation** – Spending even a few minutes daily in reflection or prayer allows you to release worries, center your mind, and open your heart to guidance.

2. **Rituals That Build Calm** – Simple actions, like lighting a candle, visiting a sacred space, or reciting affirmations, create a sense of continuity and grounding.

3. **Trust in a Higher Plan** – When intrusive thoughts or fears appear, remind yourself: "I may not understand everything, but I trust there is a path for me."

4. **Journaling for Faith** – Write down moments when you felt supported, safe, or guided. Seeing patterns of care and protection builds reassurance over time.

Integrating Faith into Daily Life

Faith is most powerful when combined with action. While prayers and rituals soothe the heart, intentional steps toward self-care, learning, and connection help translate that inner calm into daily resilience.

Exercise:

Take one recurring worry or fear and write it down. Then, write a line of faith or reassurance next to it. For example:
"*I fear she will be with someone else.*" → "*I trust that life unfolds as it should, and I am guided toward peace.*"

Over time, this practice rewires the mind to pause, acknowledge fear, and then let it rest in faith instead of spiraling endlessly.

****

"Even with faith as a guide, moments of solitude can feel lonely—but solitude also becomes a space for growth and reflection."

Chapter 18:

Loneliness vs. Solitude

"Loneliness may sting, but solitude can transform into a sanctuary for self-discovery."

There is a subtle but powerful difference between loneliness and solitude. Loneliness is the ache of missing someone, the sense of emptiness when a connection is absent. Solitude, on the other hand, is the conscious choice to be alone in order to heal, reflect, and grow.

Understanding Loneliness

When memories of the past keep replaying or thoughts of someone linger, loneliness often appears. It feels heavy, uninvited, and persistent. It can make the heart crave connection, even when it's unhealthy to seek it.

Transforming Loneliness into Solitude

Solitude is not a punishment or isolation; it is a space of empowerment. In solitude, you are free from external pressures and can engage deeply with your inner self.

Practical Steps to Embrace Solitude:

1. **Create a Safe Space** – Find a quiet corner, a journal, or a peaceful walk where you can be alone without distraction.

2. **Reflect Without Judgment** – Observe your thoughts and emotions as they arise, without labeling them as "good" or "bad."

3. **Engage in Meaningful Activities** – Use alone time to read, write, draw, or practice mindfulness. These activities anchor you in the present moment.

4. **Celebrate Your Own Company** – Practice saying, "*I am enough. My presence is valuable.*" This slowly builds self-reliance and inner calm.

The Healing Power of Solitude

When you begin to see solitude as a gift, the pain of loneliness softens. You learn to enjoy your own company, to listen to your heart, and to grow independently. The more you embrace solitude, the less the mind clings to the past or obsesses over what cannot be changed.

Exercise:

Spend 20–30 minutes in solitude today. Sit quietly, observe your thoughts, and write down any patterns that emerge. Then reflect: "*What can I learn from myself in this quiet moment?*"

Solitude is the bridge between pain and personal growth. It teaches you that being alone does not mean being lonely – it means becoming whole.

****

"Time alone and self-reflection help us redefine love, shifting from attachment to a healthier, freer understanding."

Chapter 19:

Redefining Love

"Redefining love means seeing it as freedom, respect, and inner peace rather than dependency."

Love is often misunderstood. We may associate it with longing, dependence, or the need for someone else to complete us. True love, however, begins with understanding, respect, and inner peace. Redefining love is about moving from attachment to a healthier, freer experience of connection.

Understanding Attachment vs. True Love

Attachment keeps us clinging to people, memories, or imagined outcomes. It can create anxiety, jealousy, and suffering. True love, in contrast:

- Respects boundaries
- Encourages growth, not dependence
- Brings peace rather than constant restlessness

Healing Past Attachments

Before we can embrace healthy love, we must heal the wounds of past attachments. This involves:

1. **Acknowledging Your Feelings** - Accept your emotions without judgment. Recognize what you are holding on to.

2. **Letting Go of Control** - You cannot control other people's choices or feelings. Release the need to shape their actions.

3. **Forgiving Yourself and Others** - Forgiveness is a gift that frees your heart from bitterness.

Defining Love for the Future

Redefined love is:

- **Freedom** - Giving both yourself and others space to grow.

- **Respect** - Honoring your own boundaries and those of others.

- **Inner Peace** - Feeling complete in your own presence, not relying on external validation.

Practical Exercises

1. **Reflective Journaling** – Write: "What does healthy love look like to me?"

2. **Visualization** – Imagine relationships where you and the other person feel free, supported, and respected.

3. **Affirmations** – Repeat: "I am capable of loving deeply without losing myself."

The Path Forward

By redefining love, you prepare yourself for connections that are nurturing, empowering, and lasting. You stop chasing what is not meant for you and start attracting relationships that honor your heart and mind.

Exercise:

Think of one past attachment. Write down the lessons it taught you. Then write how you would approach love now, with freedom, respect, and inner peace.

Redefining love is not about giving up on relationships — it's about giving yourself the love and respect you deserve first.

****

"Finally, armed with insight, self-awareness, and resilience, we can live forward, not backward, choosing the future over the past."

Chapter 20:

Living Forward, Not Backward

"Integration of lessons learned allows us to step confidently into the future."

The past has shaped you, but it does not define your future. Every experience, every tear, and every moment of reflection has taught you something invaluable. Living forward is about integrating those lessons and choosing a life guided by awareness, purpose, and hope.

Why Moving Forward Matters

When we dwell in the past, we carry its weight into the present, slowing our growth and clouding our joy. Moving forward doesn't mean forgetting; it means learning to live with wisdom, not regret.

Steps to Living Forward

1. **Acknowledge the Lessons** – Reflect on what your experiences have taught you. Recognize your growth.

2. **Set Intentional Goals** – Decide what kind of life you want to create. Focus on actions that align with your values.

3. **Release What You Cannot Change** – Let go of guilt, resentment, or "what could have been." Peace comes when you stop trying to rewrite the past.

4. **Embrace Change** – Life moves, and so should you. Accept new opportunities, relationships, and challenges with an open heart.

Practices to Stay Forward-Focused

- **Daily Reflection** – Spend a few minutes journaling about what you are grateful for today and what steps you took toward your goals.

- **Mindful Presence** – Focus on the present moment. Notice sights, sounds, and feelings without judgment.

- **Vision Crafting** – Create a vision board or mental image of the life you want, and revisit it regularly to stay motivated.

From Healing to Thriving

The journey through heartbreak, fear, and longing was not in vain. You have learned how to process emotions, honor your heart, and trust yourself. Now, you can turn that wisdom into a life that is not just about surviving, but thriving.

💡 **Exercise:**

Write down three things you want to achieve in the next six months. For each, note one small action you can take today to move closer to it. This turns intention into momentum.

Closing Thought

Living forward is a conscious choice. It's about embracing the unknown with courage, letting go of what no longer serves you, and welcoming a future shaped by your own resilience, love, and wisdom.

****

"And beyond these pages, practical exercises, journaling prompts, and personal rituals can help you reinforce the lessons learned and carry this healing into every day of your life."

"With your heart stronger, your mind clearer, and your perspective reshaped, it's now your turn to take action. Use these reflections, exercises, and rituals to continue your journey, turning insight into lasting change and freedom."

Reflection & Next Steps

Purpose: Give readers a concrete way to apply the lessons and continue their healing journey.

Reflection Questions:

- Which chapter resonated most with you and why?
- Which recurring thoughts or emotional loops do you notice in your own life?
- How can you apply the exercises or practices from the book to your daily routine?

Practical Actions:

1. **Journaling:** Write a letter to yourself summarizing what you've learned.
2. **Affirmations:** Create 3 daily affirmations about self-worth, trust, and love.

3. **Daily Mindfulness:** Spend 5–10 minutes noticing your thoughts without judgment.

4. **Ritual of Renewal:** Pick one meaningful day each month to reflect, release, and set intentions.

Closing Note:

Healing is not a linear path. Some days will feel heavier, others lighter. But with awareness, faith, and self-kindness, you can gradually move from heartache to a space of inner strength and freedom.

9 788198 195449

Printed at Repro India Ltd.